Math Workbooks 3rd Grade:

Fractions

(Baby Professor Learning Books)

Comparing Proper Fractions

Compare the fractions, and write > or < or = between them.

1. $\dfrac{2}{3}$ ☐ $\dfrac{4}{8}$

2. $\dfrac{3}{6}$ ☐ $\dfrac{1}{4}$

3. $\dfrac{3}{6}$ ☐ $\dfrac{4}{8}$

4. $\dfrac{1}{4}$ ☐ $\dfrac{2}{6}$

5. $\dfrac{1}{3}$ ☐ $\dfrac{2}{5}$

6. $\dfrac{4}{7}$ ☐ $\dfrac{1}{5}$

7.

$$\frac{4}{8} \ \Box \ \frac{2}{3}$$

8.

$$\frac{3}{7} \ \Box \ \frac{1}{5}$$

9.

$$\frac{2}{3} \ \Box \ \frac{3}{8}$$

10.

$$\frac{2}{5} \ \Box \ \frac{4}{8}$$

11.

$$\frac{2}{8} \ \Box \ \frac{4}{7}$$

12.

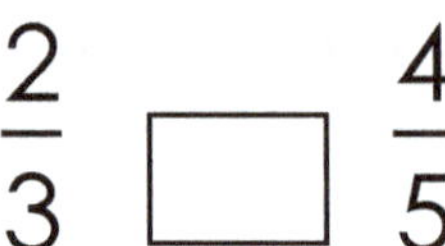

$$\frac{3}{7} \ \Box \ \frac{4}{5}$$

13.

$$\frac{2}{3} \ \Box \ \frac{4}{5}$$

14.

$$\frac{7}{8} \ \Box \ \frac{3}{4}$$

15.

$$\frac{4}{7} \ \Box \ \frac{6}{8}$$

16.

$$\frac{1}{3} \ \Box \ \frac{3}{7}$$

17. $\dfrac{5}{7}$ ⬚ $\dfrac{2}{6}$

18. $\dfrac{2}{8}$ ⬚ $\dfrac{3}{5}$

19. $\dfrac{2}{5}$ ⬚ $\dfrac{6}{7}$

20. $\dfrac{2}{4}$ ⬚ $\dfrac{1}{3}$

21. $\dfrac{3}{7}$ ⬚ $\dfrac{5}{8}$

22. $\dfrac{4}{8}$ ⬚ $\dfrac{3}{4}$

23. $\dfrac{2}{6}$ ⬚ $\dfrac{5}{7}$

24. $\dfrac{5}{6}$ ⬚ $\dfrac{6}{7}$

25. $\dfrac{3}{8}$ ⬚ $\dfrac{6}{7}$

26. $\dfrac{4}{6}$ ⬚ $\dfrac{3}{5}$

27. $\dfrac{4}{7}$ $\square$ $\dfrac{1}{4}$

28. $\dfrac{5}{8}$ $\square$ $\dfrac{3}{7}$

29. $\dfrac{2}{5}$ $\square$ $\dfrac{1}{3}$

30. $\dfrac{3}{7}$ $\square$ $\dfrac{1}{4}$

31. $\dfrac{4}{6}$ $\square$ $\dfrac{1}{3}$

32. $\dfrac{5}{7}$ $\square$ $\dfrac{4}{8}$

33. $\dfrac{7}{8}$ $\square$ $\dfrac{4}{7}$

34. $\dfrac{4}{8}$ $\square$ $\dfrac{1}{6}$

35. $\dfrac{1}{5}$ $\square$ $\dfrac{4}{8}$

36. $\dfrac{5}{8}$ $\square$ $\dfrac{3}{6}$

37.

$\frac{3}{6}$ ☐ $\frac{6}{7}$

38.

$\frac{3}{4}$ ☐ $\frac{1}{3}$

39.

$\frac{5}{8}$ ☐ $\frac{3}{5}$

40.

$\frac{4}{6}$ ☐ $\frac{3}{4}$

41.

$\frac{2}{6}$ ☐ $\frac{4}{5}$

42.

$\frac{5}{7}$ ☐ $\frac{4}{5}$

43.

$\frac{5}{6}$ ☐ $\frac{2}{4}$

44.

$\frac{4}{7}$ ☐ $\frac{7}{8}$

45.

$\frac{3}{6}$ ☐ $\frac{1}{4}$

Comparing Improper Fractions

Compare the fractions, and write > or < or = between them.

1. $\dfrac{5}{4}$ ☐ $\dfrac{6}{7}$

2. $\dfrac{4}{7}$ ☐ $\dfrac{2}{6}$

3. $\dfrac{1}{5}$ ☐ $\dfrac{4}{6}$

4. $\dfrac{5}{6}$ ☐ $\dfrac{1}{3}$

5. $\dfrac{5}{4}$ ☐ $\dfrac{7}{5}$

6. $\dfrac{3}{7}$ ☐ $\dfrac{4}{6}$

7. $\dfrac{3}{5}$ ☐ $\dfrac{4}{8}$

8. $\dfrac{6}{7}$ ☐ $\dfrac{3}{6}$

9. $\dfrac{5}{7}$ ☐ $\dfrac{6}{5}$

10. $\dfrac{5}{7}$ ☐ $\dfrac{3}{5}$

11. $\dfrac{7}{3}$ ☐ $\dfrac{8}{4}$

12. $\dfrac{7}{6}$ ☐ $\dfrac{4}{5}$

13. $\dfrac{5}{4}$ ☐ $\dfrac{7}{8}$

14. $\dfrac{6}{5}$ ☐ $\dfrac{5}{7}$

15. $\dfrac{5}{3}$ ☐ $\dfrac{8}{5}$

16. $\dfrac{3}{2}$ ☐ $\dfrac{4}{3}$

17. $\dfrac{4}{7}$ ☐ $\dfrac{3}{5}$

18. $\dfrac{4}{3}$ ☐ $\dfrac{7}{6}$

19. $\dfrac{7}{4}$ ☐ $\dfrac{2}{1}$

20. $\dfrac{2}{3}$ ☐ $\dfrac{6}{7}$

21. $\dfrac{2}{5}$ ☐ $\dfrac{1}{6}$

22. $\dfrac{2}{6}$ ☐ $\dfrac{1}{8}$

23. $\dfrac{3}{5}$ ☐ $\dfrac{1}{8}$

24. $\dfrac{5}{6}$ ☐ $\dfrac{8}{7}$

25. $\dfrac{2}{3}$ ☐ $\dfrac{5}{6}$

26. $\dfrac{8}{4}$ ☐ $\dfrac{5}{2}$

27. $\dfrac{2}{8}$ ☐ $\dfrac{4}{7}$

28. $\dfrac{7}{8}$ ☐ $\dfrac{2}{5}$

29. $\dfrac{6}{8}$ ☐ $\dfrac{2}{3}$

30. $\dfrac{1}{4}$ ☐ $\dfrac{2}{8}$

31. $\dfrac{3}{5}$ ☐ $\dfrac{7}{8}$

32. $\dfrac{8}{7}$ ☐ $\dfrac{7}{8}$

33. $\dfrac{4}{7}$ ☐ $\dfrac{1}{3}$

34. $\dfrac{2}{4}$ ☐ $\dfrac{4}{6}$

35. $\dfrac{7}{5}$ ☐ $\dfrac{8}{6}$

36. $\dfrac{5}{8}$ ☐ $\dfrac{2}{3}$

37. $\dfrac{6}{4}$ ☐ $\dfrac{8}{7}$

38. $\dfrac{1}{3}$ ☐ $\dfrac{3}{6}$

39. $\dfrac{2}{1}$ ☐ $\dfrac{7}{3}$

40. $\dfrac{4}{8}$ ☐ $\dfrac{2}{3}$

41. $\dfrac{1}{3}$ ☐ $\dfrac{2}{8}$

42. $\dfrac{3}{7}$ ☐ $\dfrac{5}{6}$

43. $\dfrac{5}{6}$ ☐ $\dfrac{3}{8}$

44. $\dfrac{1}{5}$ ☐ $\dfrac{2}{7}$

45. $\dfrac{1}{8}$ ☐ $\dfrac{3}{6}$

Adding Proper Fractions

Solve.

1. $\dfrac{7}{3} + \dfrac{5}{3} =$

2. $\dfrac{8}{6} + \dfrac{3}{6} =$

3. $\dfrac{2}{5} + \dfrac{4}{5} =$

4. $\dfrac{11}{12} + \dfrac{10}{12} =$

5. $\dfrac{11}{10} + \dfrac{6}{10} =$

6. $\dfrac{7}{3} + \dfrac{1}{3} =$

7. $\dfrac{10}{3} + \dfrac{4}{3} =$

8. $\dfrac{7}{6} + \dfrac{1}{6} =$

9. $\dfrac{1}{2} + \dfrac{11}{2} =$

10. $\dfrac{10}{3} + \dfrac{10}{3} =$

11. $\dfrac{8}{6} + \dfrac{1}{6} =$

12. $\dfrac{10}{9} + \dfrac{2}{9} =$

13. $\dfrac{1}{5} + \dfrac{1}{5} =$

14. $\dfrac{2}{6} + \dfrac{7}{6} =$

15. $\dfrac{5}{7} + \dfrac{1}{7} =$

16. $\dfrac{4}{10} + \dfrac{6}{10} =$

17. $\dfrac{3}{10} + \dfrac{9}{10} =$

18. $\dfrac{10}{3} + \dfrac{11}{3} =$

19. $\dfrac{5}{10} + \dfrac{4}{10} =$

20. $\dfrac{7}{10} + \dfrac{8}{10} =$

Adding Fractions
with Pie Charts

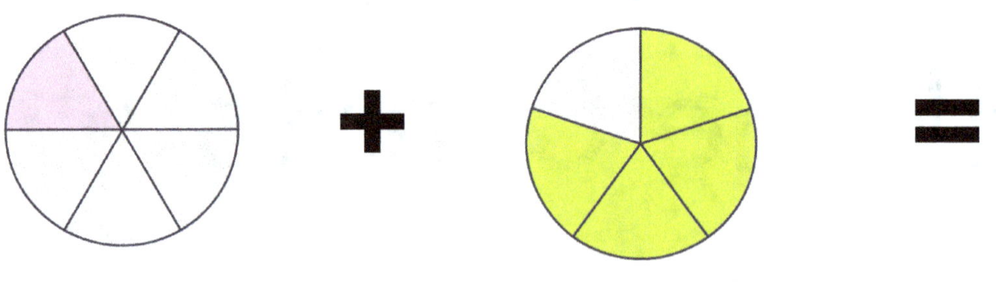

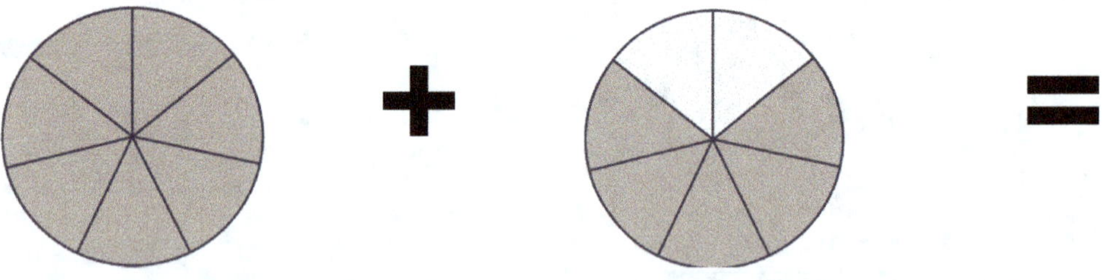

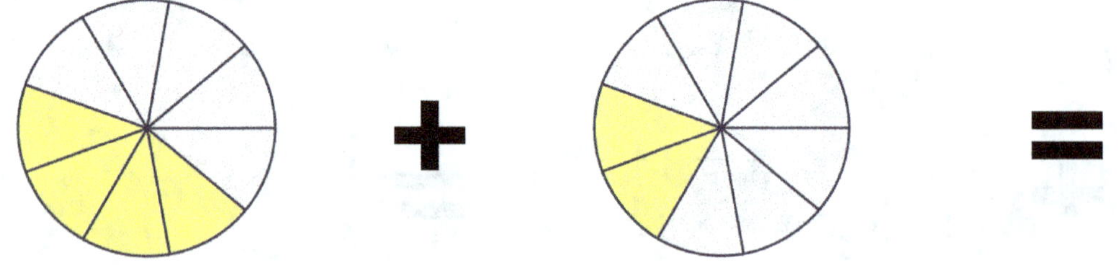

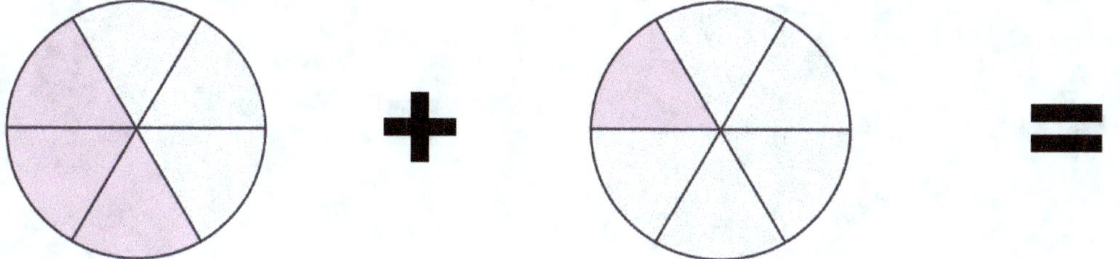

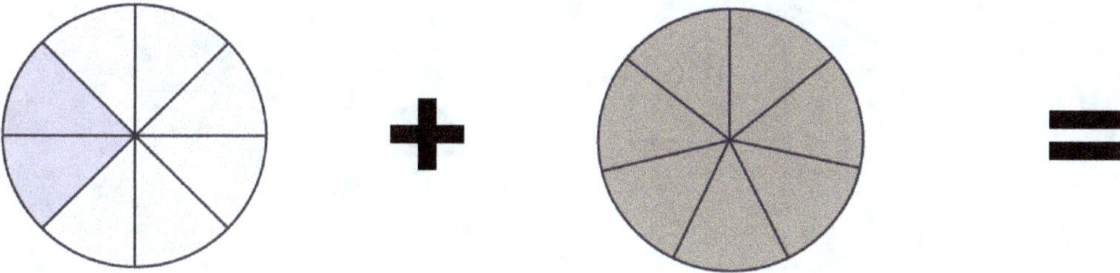

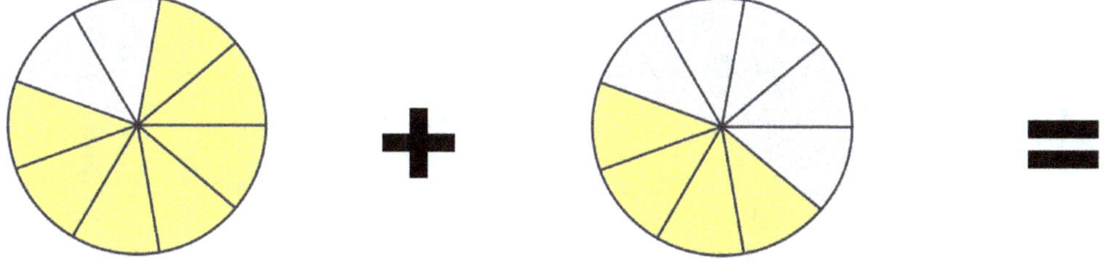

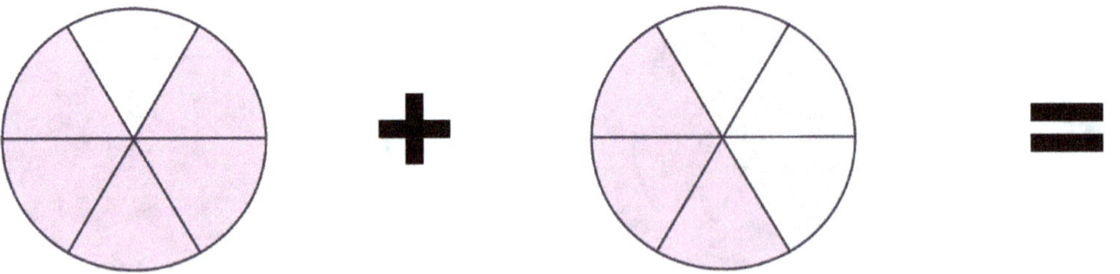

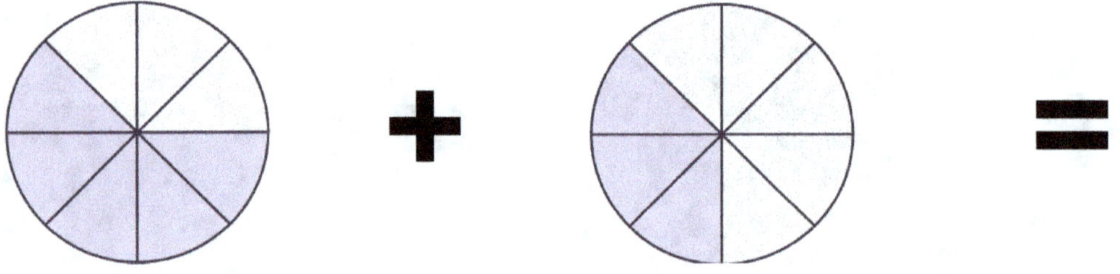

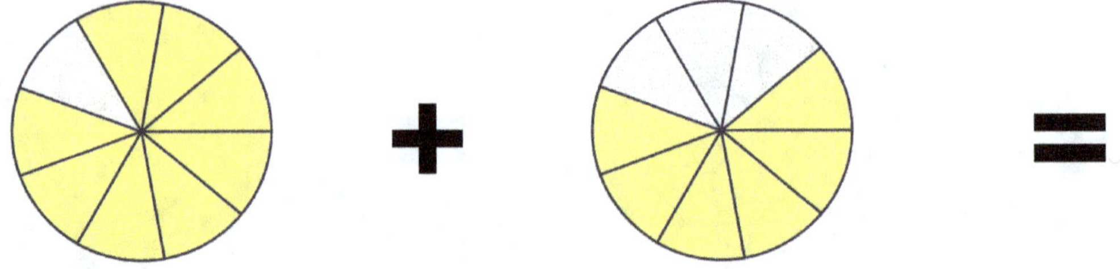

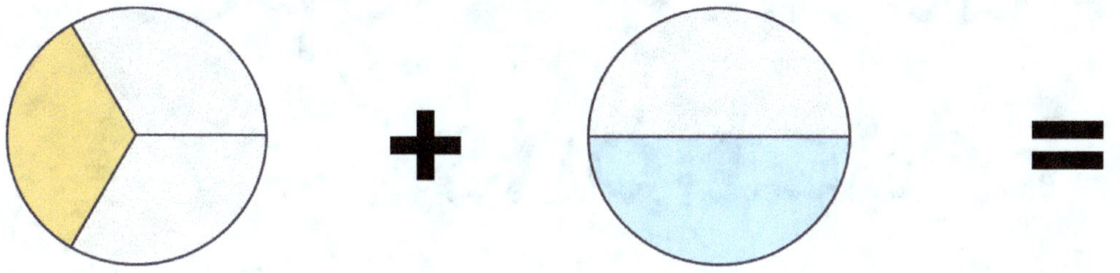

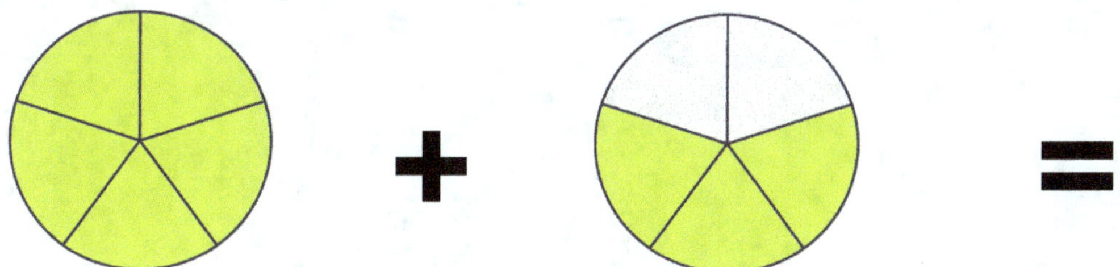

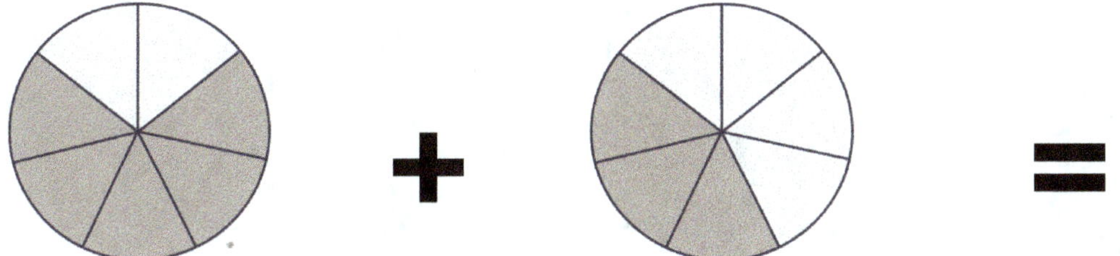

Subtracting Proper Fractions

Solve.

1. $\dfrac{4}{8} - \dfrac{1}{8} =$

2. $\dfrac{5}{8} - \dfrac{2}{8} =$

3. $\dfrac{6}{10} - \dfrac{5}{10} =$

4. $\dfrac{11}{4} - \dfrac{11}{4} =$

5. $\dfrac{8}{7} - \dfrac{4}{7} =$

6. $\dfrac{7}{2} - \dfrac{5}{2} =$

7. $\dfrac{9}{4} - \dfrac{1}{4} =$

8. $\dfrac{9}{6} - \dfrac{5}{6} =$

9. $\dfrac{3}{6} - \dfrac{2}{6} =$

10. $\dfrac{12}{3} - \dfrac{11}{3} =$

11. $\dfrac{11}{9} - \dfrac{7}{9} =$

12. $\dfrac{11}{6} - \dfrac{4}{6} =$

13. $\dfrac{8}{12} - \dfrac{8}{12} =$

14. $\dfrac{11}{10} - \dfrac{3}{10} =$

15. $\dfrac{12}{8} - \dfrac{3}{8} =$

16. $\dfrac{7}{11} - \dfrac{4}{11} =$

17. $\dfrac{1}{9} - \dfrac{1}{9} =$

18. $\dfrac{10}{7} - \dfrac{8}{7} =$

19. $\dfrac{8}{7} - \dfrac{4}{7} =$

20. $\dfrac{11}{4} - \dfrac{7}{4} =$

21. $\dfrac{12}{11} - \dfrac{12}{11} =$

22. $\dfrac{7}{2} - \dfrac{5}{2} =$

23. $\dfrac{9}{12} - \dfrac{7}{12} =$

24. $\dfrac{9}{3} - \dfrac{1}{3} =$

25. $\dfrac{12}{6} - \dfrac{3}{6} =$

26. $\dfrac{10}{3} - \dfrac{4}{3} =$

27. $\dfrac{4}{5} - \dfrac{1}{5} =$

28. $\dfrac{5}{11} - \dfrac{5}{11} =$

29. $\dfrac{12}{10} - \dfrac{2}{10} =$

30. $\dfrac{12}{10} - \dfrac{11}{10} =$

Fractions to Decimals Conversion

Solve.

1. 33/50

2. 3 4/5

3. 7 47/50

4. 9/125

5. 1 49/50

6. 13/20

7. 1/10

8. 91/100

9. 107/1000

10. 14 9/10

11. 41 1/2

12. 197/500

13. 401/500

14. 1/2

15. 7/8

16. 167/1000

17. 333/1000

18. 833/1000

19. 1/8

20. 5/8

21. 667/1000

22. 4/5

23. 2/5

24. 3/5

25. 1/4

26. 667/1000

27. 3/4

28. 1/5

29. 333/1000

30. 5/16

Score Sheet

Comparing Proper Fractions	/45
Comparing Improper Fractions	/45
Adding Proper Fractions	/20
Adding Fractions with Pie Charts	/15
Subtracting Proper Fractions	/30
Fractions to Decimal Conversion	/30
TOTAL	**/185**

Congratulations!

Completion Certificate

is awarded to

____

1.   >
2.   >
3.   =
4.   <
5.   <
6.   >
7.   <
8.   >
9.   >
10. <
11. <
12. <
13. <
14. >
15. <
16. <
17. >
18. <
19. <
20. >
21. <
22. <
23. <

24. <
25. <
26. >
27. >
28. >
29. >
30. >
31. >
32. >
33. >
34. >
35. <
36. >
37. <
38. >
39. >
40. <
41. <
42. <
43. >
44. <
45. >

1.   >
2.   >

3.   <
4.   >

5.   <
6.   <
7.   >
8.   >
9.   <
10.   >
11.   >
12.   >
13.   >
14.   >
15.   >
16.   >
17.   <
18.   >
19.   <
20.   <
21.   >
22.   >
23.   >
24.   <
25.   <

26.   <
27.   <
28.   >
29.   >
30.   =
31.   <
32.   >
33.   >
34.   <
35.   >
36.   <
37.   >
38.   <
39.   <
40.   <
41.   >
42.   <
43.   >
44.   <
45.   <

1.   4
2.   11/6 or 1 5/6
3.   6/5 or 1 1/5

4.   21/12 or 1 3/4
5.   17/10 or 1 7/10
6.   8/3 or 2 2/3

7.   14/3 or 4 2/3
8.   8/6 or 1 1/3
9.   12/2 or 6
10.   20/3 or 6 2/3
11.   9/6 or 1 1/2
12.   12/9 or 1 1/3
13.   2/5

14.   9/6 or 1 1/2
15.   6/7
16.   1
17.   12/10 or 1 1/5
18.   7
19.   9/10
20.   15/10 or 1 1/2

1.   1/4 + 2/3 = 11/12
2.   4/6 + 2/6 = 6/6 or 1
3.   4/8 + 2/8 = 6/8 or 3/4
4.   1/6 + 4/5 = 29/30
5.   7/7 + 5/7 = 12/7 or 1 5/7
6.   4/9 + 2/9 = 6/9 or 2/3
7.   3/6 + 1/6 = 4/6 or 2/3
8.   2/8 + 7/7 = 5/4 or 1 1/4

9.   7/9 + 4/9 = 11/9 or 1 2/9
10.   5/6 + 3/6 = 8/6 or 1 1/3
11.   5/8 + 3/8 = 8/8 or 1
12.   8/9 + 6/9 = 14/9 or 1 2/3
13.   1/3 + 1/2 = 5/6
14.   5/5 + 3/5 = 8/5 or 1 3/5
15.   5/7 + 3/7 = 8/7 or 1 1/7

1.   1. 3/8
2.   2. 3/8
3.   3. 1/10
4.   4. 0
5.   5. 3/7
6.   6. 1
7.   7. 2

8.   8 2/3
9.   9. 1/6
10.   10. 1/3
11.   11. 4/9
12.   12. 7/6 or 1 1/6
13.   13. 0
14.   14. 4/5

15.   15. 9/8 or 1 1/8
16.   16. 3/11
17.   17. 0
18.   18. 2/7
19.   19. 4/7
20.   20. 1
21.   21. 0
22.   22. 1

23.   23. 1/6
24.   24. 8/3 or 2 2/3
25.   25. 9/6 or 1 1/2
26.   26. 2
27.   27. 3/5
28.   28. 0
29.   29. 1
30.   30. 1/10

1.   0.66
2.   3.8
3.   7.94
4.   0.072
5.   1.98
6.   0.65
7.   .1
8.   0.91
9.   0.107
10.   14.9
11.   41.5
12.   0.394
13.   0.802
14.   0.5
15.   0.875
16.   0.167

17.   0.333
18.   0.833
19.   0.125
20.   0.625
21.   0.667
22.   0.8
23.   0.4
24.   0.6
25.   0.25
26.   0.667
27.   0.75
28.   0.2
29.   0.333
30.   0.3125